THE LAST CAT BOOK

THE LAST CAT BOOK

Robert E. Howard
Illustrated by Peter Kuper

DODD, MEAD & COMPANY
NEW YORK

Library of Congress Cataloging in Publication Data:

Howard, Robert Ervin, 1906–1936.
  The last cat book.

  1. Howard, Robert Ervin, 1906–1936—Biography.
2. Authors, American—20th century—Biography.
3. Cats. I. Title.
PS3515.0842Z468 1984   813'.52   84-3974
ISBN 0-396-08370-6

The text of this work originally appeared in *The Howard Collector*, Autumn 1971 issue, under the title of "The Beast from the Abyss," and was subsequently included in THE HOWARD COLLECTOR, edited by Glen Lord and published by Ace Books, 1979.

DEDICATED TO

TONY AND ROSE

here is something particularly harrowing about the sight of an animal in pain; a desperate despair, undiluted by hope or reason, that makes it, in a way, a more awful and tragic sight than that of an injured human. In the agony cry of a cat all the blind abysmal anguish of the black cosmic pits seems concentrated.

t is a scream from the jungle, the death howl of a past unspeakably distant, forgotten, and denied by humanity, yet which still lies like a sleeping shadow at the back of the subconscious, to be awakened into shuddering memory by a pain-edge yell from a bestial mouth.

ot only in agony and death is the cat a reminder of that brutish past. In his anger cries and his love cries, his gliding course through the grass, the hunger that burns shamelessly from his slitted eyes, in all his movements and actions is advertised his kinship with the wild, his tamelessness, and his contempt for man.

 nferior to the dog the cat is, nevertheless, more like human beings than is the former. For he is vain yet servile, greedy yet fastidious, lazy, lustful, and selfish.

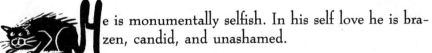 He is monumentally selfish. In his self love he is bra-zen, candid, and unashamed.

iving nothing in return, he demands everything—and demands it in a rasping, hungry, whining squall that seems to tremble with self-pity, and accuse the world at large of perfidy and a broken contract.

 His eyes are suspicious and avaricious, the eyes of a miser.

 is manner is at once arrogant and debased.

He arches his back and rubs himself against humanity's leg, dirging a doleful plea, while his eyes glare threats and his claws slide convulsively in and out of their padded sheaths.

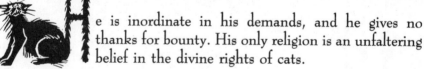He is inordinate in his demands, and he gives no thanks for bounty. His only religion is an unfaltering belief in the divine rights of cats.

he dog exists only for man, man exists only for cats.

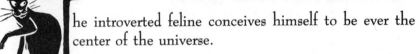 The introverted feline conceives himself to be ever the center of the universe.

 n his narrow skull there is no room for the finer feelings.

ull a drowning kitten out of the gutter and provide him with a soft cushion to sleep upon, and cream as often as he desires. Shelter, pamper, and coddle him all his useless and self-centered life. What will he give you in return? He will allow you to stroke his fur; he will bestow upon you a condescending purr, after the manner of one conferring a great favor. There the evidences of his gratitude end.

Your house may burn over your head, thugs may break in, rape your wife, knock Uncle Theobald in the head, and string you up by your thumbs to make you reveal the whereabouts of your hoarded wealth. The average dog would die in the defense even of Uncle Theobald.

ut your fat and pampered feline will look on without interest; he will make no exertions in your behalf, and after the fray, will, likely as not, make a hearty meal off your unprotected corpse.

am not a victim of the peculiar cat-phobia which afflicts some people, neither am I one of those whose fondness for the animals is as inexplicable and tyrannical in its way as the above mentioned repulsion. I can take cats or leave them alone.

n my childhood I was ordinarily surrounded by cats. Occasionally they were given to me; more often they simply drifted in and settled. Sometimes they drifted out just as mysteriously. I am speaking of ordinary cats, country cats, alley cats, cats without pedigree or pride of ancestry. Mongrel animals, like mongrel people, are by far the most interesting as a study.

n my part of the country, high-priced, pure-blooded felines were unknown until a comparatively recent date. Such terms as Persians, Angoras, Maltese, Manx, and the like, meant little or nothing. A cat was a cat, and classified only according to its ability to catch mice.

or myself, give me an alley cat every time.

 remember with what intense feelings of disgust I viewed the first thoroughbred cat I ever saw—a cumbersome ball of gray fur, with the wide blank stare of utter stupidity.

dog came barking wildly across the yard, the pampered aristocrat goggled dumbly, then lumbered across the porch and attempted to climb a post. An alley cat would have shot up that shaft like a streak of gray lightning, to turn at a vantage point and spit down evil vituperation on its enemy's head. This blundering inbred monster tumbled ignominiously from the column and sprawled—*on its back* —in front of the dog, who was so astounded by the phenomenon that it evidently concluded that its prey was not a cat after all, and hastily took itself off. It was not the first time that a battle was won by awkward stupidity.

once lived on a farm infested by rats beyond description. They broke up setting hens, devoured eggs and small chickens, and gnawed holes in the floor of the house. The building was old, the floors rotten. The rats played havoc with them. I nailed strips of tin over the holes they gnawed, and in the night I could hear their teeth grating on the tin, and their squeals of rage. Traps proved ineffectual. Rats are wise, not so easily snared as mice.

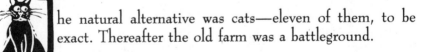
he natural alternative was cats—eleven of them, to be exact. Thereafter the old farm was a battleground.

The big gray wharf rats, as we called them, are no mean foes for a cat. More than once I have seen one of them defeat a full-grown feline in pitched battle. The ferocity of the cornered rat is proverbial, and unlike many such proverbs, borne out by actuality.

The most valiant of all the crew was a gray cat of medium size called, through some obscure process, Fessler. Despite the fact that he was once ignominiously routed by a giant rat in a Homeric battle that should have formed the base for a whole cycle of rodent hero-sagas, he was a cat among cats. In him, fantastic as it may seem, I sometimes seemed to detect a fleeting shadow of an emotion that was almost affection.

He had poise and dignity; most cats have these qualities. He had courage—for which, despite legends to the contrary, the feline race in general is not noted. He was a mouser of note. He was intelligent—the most intelligent cat I have ever known.

n the end, when all the cats but one died in one of those unexplainable plagues that strikes communities of felines, he dragged himself back to the house to die. Stricken, he had retired to the barn, and there he fought out his losing battle alone; but with death on him, he tottered from his retreat, staggered painfully through the night, and sank down beneath my window, where his body was found the next morning. It was as if, in his last extremity, he sought the human aid that mere instinct could not have prompted him to seek.

ost of the other cats died in solitary refuges of their own. One, a black kitten, recovered, but was so thin and weak it could not stand. My cousin shot a rabbit, cut it up, and fed the cat the raw meat. Unable to stand, it crouched above the warm flesh, ate enough to have burst a well cat, then, turning on its side, smiled as plainly as any human ever smiles, and sank into death like one falling asleep.

t has been my misfortune to see many animals die, but I never saw a more peaceful, contented death than that. May my own death be as easy as that cat's!

said one cat lived. For all I know, she may be living yet, populating the mesquite-grown hills with her progeny. For she was a veritable phoenix of a cat, defying death, and rising from the ruins of catdom unharmed, and generally with a fresh litter of squalling young.

She was large of body, variegated of color—a somewhat confusing mixture of white, yellow, and black. Her face was dusky, so she was named Blackface.

She had a sister, a smaller cat, who seemed borne down by the woes of the world. Her face was the comically tragic mask of a weary clown. She died in the Big Plague.

lackface did not die. Just before the cats began to fall, she vanished, and I supposed that she had been stricken and dragged herself away to die in the bushes. But I was mistaken. After the last of her companions had been gathered to their ancestors, after the polluted gathering places had been cleaned by time and the elements, Blackface came home. With her came a brood of long-legged kittens. She remained at the farm until the youngsters were ready to wean, then once more she disappeared. When she returned, a few weeks later, she returned alone.

had begun to accumulate cats again, and as long as I lived on the farm, I enjoyed periods of cat-inflation, separated by times during which the mysterious plague returned and wiped them out. But the plague never got Blackface. Somehow, that she-cat knew, and avoided the doom that struck down her companions.

She was taciturn, cryptic, laden with mysterious wisdom older than Egypt.

She did not raise her kittens about her. I think that she had learned there was danger in thickly populated centers. Always, when they were able to fend for themselves, she led them into the woods and lost them. And however impossible it may be for a human being to "lose" a cat, none of them ever came back to the farm from which Blackface led them. But the countryside began to be infested with "wild" cats.

er sons and daughters dwelt in the mesquite flats, in the chaparral, and among the cactus beds. Some few of them took up at farmhouses and became mousers of fame; but most of them remained untamed, hunters and slayers, devourers of birds and rodents and young rabbits, and, I suspect, of chickens.

lackface was cloaked in mystery. She came in the night, and in the night she went. She bore her kittens in the deep woods, brought them back to civilization for a space that they might be sheltered while in their helpless infancy—and that her own work might be less arduous—and back to the woods she took them when the time was ripe.

s the years passed, her returns to civilization became less and less frequent. At last she did not even bring her brood, but supported them in the wilderness. The primitive called her, and the call was stronger than the urge to slothful ease. She was silent, primordial, drawn to the wild. She came no more to the dwellings of man, but I had glimpses of her at dawn or twilight, flashing like a streak of black-barred gold through the tall grass, or gliding phantom-like through the mesquites.

The fire in her elemental eyes was undimmed, the muscles rippling under her fur unsoftened by age. That was nearly twenty years ago. It would not surprise me to learn that she still lives among the cactus-grown valleys and the mesquite-clad hills. Some things are too elemental to die.

 ust now I am uncertain as to the number of cats I possess.

I am uncertain as to their numbers, because there has been an addition to the community, and I do not know how many. I hear them squalling among the hay bales, but I have not had an opportunity to count them. I know only that they are the offspring of a stocky, lazy gray cat, whose democratic mongrel blood is diluted with some sort of thoroughbred stock.

At one time there were five. One was a black and white cat whose visits were furtive and soon ceased. One was a gray and white female, undersized, as so many good mousers are, and like a good killer, possessed of a peculiarly thin whining voice. Because of her preference to the sheds and feed stalls, she bore the casual name of Barn-cat. Another was a magnificent image of primitive savagery—a giant yellow cat, mainly a half-breed mongrel mixed with some stock that might have been Persian. So he was referred to as "the Persian."

have found that the average yellow cat is deficient in courage. The Persian was an exception. He was the biggest, most powerful mixed-breed I ever saw, and the fiercest. He was always ravenous, and his powerful jaws crushed chicken bones in a startling manner. He ate, indeed, more like a dog than a cat. He was not indolent or fastidious. He was a lusty soldier of fortune, without morals or scruples, but possessed of an enviable vitality.

He was enamored of Barn-cat, and no woman could have acted the coquette with greater perfection. She treated him like a dog. He wooed her in his most ingratiating manner, to be rewarded by spitting abuse and scratches. A lion in his dealings with members of his own sex, he was a lamb with Barn-cat.

et him approach her in the most respectable manner, and she was transformed into a spitting, clawing fury. Then when he retired discouraged, she invariably followed him, picking at him, teasing him, and giving him no peace of mind. Yet if he took hope and attempted any advances on the ground of her actions, she instantly assumed the part of an insulted virgin and greeted him with bared teeth and claws.

heir romance was not so very different from some human romances, and like all romances, came to its end. The Persian was a fighter. So much of his time was spent recovering from wounds, that he was always gaunt, and there were always several partly healed scars on his head and body. Finally he limped in with fresh wounds and a broken leg. He lay around for a short time, refusing assistance, and then disappeared. I think that, following his instincts, he dragged himself away somewhere to die.

Barn-cat's career was short. Soon after her lover met his end, she appeared one morning with her tail almost chewed off close to her body. Doubtless she had internal wounds. She was the only one of the crew worth her salt as a mouser, and while she normally avoided the big gray rats, I believe they were at last responsible for her doom. At any rate, she too vanished with her wounds and did not return.

he life of a cat is not numbered by nine. Usually it is short, violent, and tragic. He suffers, and makes others suffer if he can. He is primitive, bestially selfish. He is, in short, a creature of terrible and awful potentialities, a crystalization of primordial self-love, a materialization of the blackness and squalor of the abyss.

He is a green-eyed, steel-thewed, fur-clad block of darkness hewed from the Pits which know not light, nor sympathy, nor dreams, nor hope, nor beauty, nor anything except hunger and the satiating of hunger. But he has dwelt with man since the beginning, and when the last man lies down and dies, a cat will watch his throes, and likelier than not, will gorge its abysmal hunger on his cooling flesh.

ROBERT E. HOWARD (1906—1936) spent most of his life in Cross Plains, Texas, where he wrote hundreds of stories—westerns, pirate tales, historical adventures, humor, and fantasy—before taking his life, grief-stricken by the impending death of his mother. The popularity of his most famous creation, Conan of Cimmeria, and the many volumes of his work in print are a testament to the importance of his contribution to fantastic literature.

PETER KUPER was born in 1958 and grew up in Cleveland, Ohio, where he became an avid fan of comic illustrations. In 1977 he moved to New York to pursue an art career. He attended Pratt Institute for four years and successfully avoided any degree. Peter's work appears regularly in *The New York Times Book Review*, *Forbes*, *Heavy Metal*, and *Twilight Zone*.